Continuous Dreams:

Brylen's Book of Poetry

by

Brylen Jabrie Hubbell

RoseDog Books
PITTSBURGH, PENNSYLVANIA 15238

RoseDog Books
585 Alpha Drive
Suite 103
Pittsburgh, PA 15238
Visit our website at *www.rosedogbookstore.com*

ISBN: 979-8-88812-429-1
eISBN: 979-8-88812-929-6

Continuous Dreams:

Brylen's Book of Poetry

I Know What I was Born to Do

I know what I was born to do
Help make the world anew
Reveal the new and old
The greatest story ever told

Help people find their way
Make the best of today
Try to create something great
It is never too late

I feel so alive
Helping ancient things survive
I believe I was born to do this
I know I cannot resist

I know what is wrong and right
How I long to join the fight
Banish all my sorrow
And make a better tomorrow

Sister Spring

When Lady Winter takes a nap
In her silky silver cap
The warm breezes blow
And melt the shining, sparkling snow

Old friends return to sing
The arrival of Sister Spring
Tortoises and bears awake
And lap up water in the cool lake

New babies are always born
Sister Spring's dress they adorn
Prancing kits, feasting grubs
Hopping bunnies and budding shrubs

Every worm and every toad
Feels fresh in its abode
Thunder claps and rain does fall
I myself love it all

Every leaf and every clover
Celebrates the Passover
On Easter Morn when flowers nod
We're all reborn with the Lamb of God

Witches dance 'round fires hot
On the eve of Walpurgisnacht
Puppies and kitties play
Dandelions grow on May Day

Young spiders take to the sky
On their webs and breezes fly
Crickets sing with all the fairies
Rabbits feast on fresh grown berries

Birds and insects come again
A rabbit leaves its snowy den
We all welcome our cool, fresh queen,
Say hello to Sister Spring

Lord Summer

Trumpets sound in the bright warm skies
In Lord Summer flies
Dogs run and children play
During this sunny holiday

While parents try to stay cool
Kids rejoice for lack of school
There is sunshine on every heart and face
The youngest animals find their place

Clouds are scarce in the big blue sky
Americans celebrate the Fourth of July
But when the sun begins to roast
That's when you miss Lady Winter most

Still, people relax on the beach
With all of their burdens far from reach
Plants are green and bluebirds sing
To honor our Summer King!

Brother Autumn

When Lord Summer sails away
Our capricious friend comes to play
When the bear sleeps and the breeze hums
That's when Brother Autumn comes

Brother Autumn harvests corn
Wilts the rose and its pointy thorn
Shields our heads from the hot sun
Fires the leaves like the blow of a gun

Monsters, witches, and ghouls are seen
On the night of Halloween
Autumn reminds us what's worth living
On the day we call Thanksgiving

He turns the leaves gold and red
Each of us is good and fed
A cool breeze blows
Warms your heart and tickles your nose

Autumn has some beasts to keep
In the misty realms of sleep
When the good year nears its bottom,
Say hello to Brother Autumn!

Lady Winter

Heed the Lady Winter pale
In her glittering frosty vale
The world is conquered by ice
Make sure to curl up warm and nice

There's a certain stillness that winter brings
That is not found in summers or springs
It is the time when church bells ring
It is the time when angels sing

Lady Winter stretches her mighty hand
Over the water and over the land
Snow is falling everywhere
Bears are sleeping without care

Some folks love her silver night
Her sparkling trees of snowy white
Others fear her raging storm
And try to keep their families warm

Her sweeping gown blocks out the sun
Her wonder entrances everyone
Her magic wand ices the seas
Everyone tries not to freeze

Christmastide is coming near
Trailing behind is the New Year
The chill wind blows so cool
On the ancient night of Yule

Yes, she can be full of danger
Her raging storms cause much anger
But there's something we all know
When it comes her time to go
We'll greatly miss her sparkling snow

So when Lady Winter comes again,
Let's all welcome our old friend!

The Twilight and Night

As the daytime blue fades into softer gold and red
As all the youngest children should probably get to bed
I sing this song to all the lovers of the night
Her time has come, she is here, the lovely twilight

Moon of pearl and midnight sky of ink
Night is the perfect time to stay awake and think
It is the perfect time to fall asleep and dream
To frolic through the starlit land and capture a moonbeam

Goblins dance and ghosts come out to greet
Slumbering folks, grabbing hands and tickling feet
It is a joyous time, of thrill and delight
The sky as black as ink and the moon of shining white

Time to greet the many creatures of the night
Some gentle, sweet, and kind
Others looking for a fight
If you look, neither shall be hard to find

Nocturnal or diurnal, awake or asleep
Nighttime is a lovely time to float and lurk and creep
So when the twilight rolls around, what is it that you'll do?
I'm sure you'll have a good old time, merry through and through!

Daylight

Few people will argue when I say
Daytime is perfect for fun and play
The brother of the lovely night
Keeper of goodness and light

Frolicking through a sunlit field
Happiness will never yield
A time so full of light
Joyful faces shining bright

A time of innocence for everyone
Take a little breath of sun
You should not take for granted the day
Be it December, October, or May

The time of exploration
Sunlight streams throughout the nation
Birds sing and insects fly
Lovers of light rest under the blue sky

So while the night is so inviting
With its revelry and gentle lighting
The day has lots to offer, too
A jolly time when hearts are true

Nature

As the thrasher sings in the trees
Flowers are occupied by butterflies and bees
Robins, pixies, and blue bottles fly
All the beauty could make a man cry

The calls of the wild beasts ring
The wind in the mountains begins to sing
All life, so unique and strange
Everything, yet nothing will change

Nature, my first true love
Every spider, worm, and dove
Just listen to the wolf's sweet song
A love for nature can't be wrong

Magic

Magic is in all sorts of things
Rabbits' feet and birds' wings
The crescent to the full moon
A silly beetle born in June

You may not always understand
The mystical arts that rule the land
But understanding is overrated
It makes many people become jaded

You can love without understanding
Love and magic are not demanding
Love is a sort of magic
Whether it is happy or tragic

Most likely it's a bit of both
Both love and magic require an oath
Magic and love are wild and free
Love and magic are both in me

Pins and Needles

The woman who walks among the weeds
Will not seek her earthly needs
The man who is and is not
Who lives nearby the river hot
Will band and make their world anew
Love will make them one and two

He writes and writes and writes in vain
His eyes and face are all in stain
Only she can soothe his pain

Every night she cries
Every night she dies
Her mouth sewn shut from all her fears
But his heart heals her tears

What is fake and what is fair?
You'll never know with this odd pair
The man's writing is never wrong
The mouthless woman sings her song
They were YOU all along
Still yet, they are not
Love what you have, not what you've got

Ravens and crows tell the tale
Of how Pins and Needles warn and wail
They are two but they are one
They are one but they are none
They are none but they are all
It may be YOU who gets the call!

The Great Striped Wizard

The great Striped Wizard
With a heart like a blizzard
But a fire blazing in the core
Remembers what was lost before

Friend of beast and man
Wanders the woods free like Pan
Shreds with an axe of wood
He will fight for what is good

The mage shrouded in black and gray
The best of then and of today
Will protect the sacred song
You might have known him all along

Son of the Virgo star
He comes from off afar
Replays the sacred tunes
Is adorned in sacred runes

Cloaked in shadow
Rose from stone
Clothed in leather
Bound in bone

No one can truly steal his crown
No one can withstand this wizard's frown
He fights for joy all the while
People are blessed to see his smile

Still so much to learn
Still so much to earn
The sorcerer, spirit, musician, mage
Has power in heart, wave, and page

The Rack

At night, when the world is black
I sleep and dream of my shoe rack
It may seem quite strange to you
But you would envy me if you knew

A most wondrous man sits there
A man who is kind and fair
Who is always willing to take a dare
One for whom I deeply care

The sound of his voice is quite sweet
Charms all those he meets
Whether in the garage or on the streets
He accomplishes quite gallant feats

Yes, so gallant, fair, and sweet
But what's this? Someone has stolen my seat!
Now I am far from him among the feet
I sigh and start to retreat

But then I fight and make things hard
Pay no heed to the lordly bard
But I should just sit and listen
To the beautiful words that shine and glisten

Such simple things we take for granted
He sat and sang while I just ranted
I grabbed the hand of my trusted friend
Now my troubles have met their end

The Rider

She turned to me
To see
What the rider had done

That is what he said
His atmosphere red
Persephone's son

I wanted to hear the rest
It was the best
But I could not stay

I wanted to pass the test
I wanted to have his zest
But it was the break of day

Who was the rider
A Smith, A Snider?
I do not know

Could be a Ted, Mary, or Bob
Could be a Fred, Cheri, or Rob
A Lizzy, a Casper, a Joe

I knew the man who sang the song
I have known him well and long
But I still don't know who he sang of

Or maybe the answer is in my mind
But I somehow still remain blind
Could be someone I hate or love

She turned to me
To see
What the rider had done

If this is a game
I am lame
And the Wizard has won

The Kings of Music

The ones who wear the darkest mask
Have taken on a glorious task
They shall return what is lost
They ignore its lonesome cost

In the city of beasts they got their start
Each man has a noble heart
All are wise who join this brigade
All are welcome in their shade

They recall the ancient, powerful art
To challenge this would not be smart
Others lie to have this skill
These men have it at God's will

What best suits them is white and black
The secret sinners they attack
These men are adorned in spike and ink
Into their hearts all will sink

They are masters of the metal craft
Only the best receive their draft
Their jests and joking are so jolly
To despair would be great folly

Many judge but so few seek
The wisdom that the black birds speak
They know the things revealed by sight
They have learned the secrets of the night

Now these men are like a dream
These powerful lairds so perfect seem
But no doubt they have their flaws
No flaw sways them from their cause

On solitary nights when the moon is full
Let the music fill your soul
You aren't so different, it would seem
So join the army, join the dream

Hephaestus

The mighty forger, great Hephaestus
With tongs and hammer he has blessed us
Created many a useful thing
Been through so much strife and pain

Cast out of the Heavens for no good reason
Loved by kind spirits for many a season
The gods of Olympus saw him as out of place
Then he married the goddess of grace

He who the gods tried to conceal
Worked with fire and steel
Created something real
A family, love to feel

The Wind Brothers

Here they come, hooting, howling
There they go, swooping, growling
Mischievous spirits they may be
Yet still kind-hearted and free

They are there in the cooling spring
They are present when summer starts to sing
They are here when autumn comes around
In cold winter, too, they can be found

Yes, they are always there
Always willing to take a dare

As long as you have eyes to see
The silly spirits will leave you be
As long as you have ears to hear
There's nothing you should really fear

Dionysus and Ariadne

Two unknown outcasts
Two mortals with painful pasts
Two people down and lost
Two victims of love's costs

He rose up with the ancient gods
He found respectful bows and nods
To her love seemed out of reach
Till he found her on a beach

At least once, he was dead
Life sprang from his blood so red
She had pain in her heart and in her head
Jolly revelers, they were wed

Father, mother, husband, wife
Improved their lives, improved their life
One and two, above the world
Their great love story now unfurled

Odin

To me the Allfather is no stranger
Here to protect and here to endanger
A funny, tricky man he seems
When he ventures into my dreams

With his eight-legged horse and a big black dog
He changes his course, comes out of the fog
It is best to stay on his good side
So he'll pass you by on the Wild Ride!

Vidarr

Odin's heroic son
Who dwells in a grassy field
He is the only one
To be the people's shield

Along with Váli, his brother
He will dwell in the home of the gods
Make new lives for gods and for others
Despite all of the odds

When your shoes start to weather
If you want to help my brave forefather
Please give him your old leather
It will save the world, if you bother!

The Norse Gods

Odínn, cunning and wise
Has no need for two eyes
Frigg, who often sits and cries
She forsees her son's demise

Baldr, so sweet and kind
Thor, strong in body and mind
Heimdallr, who witnesses much
Ullr, helping feet to rush

Freyja, full of magic and love
Her brother, Freyr, like a dove
Loki, mischievous little sprite
Nótt, the goddess of the night

Ægir and Rán of the seas
Making waves stirred by the breeze
Son Snær, just like snow
He needs to come so things can grow

Idunn picks apples from a tree
Her husband is the poet Bragi
Her fruit rejuvenates the old
His poetry and heart are bold

Tyr, god of blood and war
Used to battles full of gore
His wife is unknown
No one knows who shares his throne

Do not go, wait! There's more
The goddess Sif is the wife of Thor
Golden hair and golden grain
Golden crop and golden mane

Vidarr, who survives the end
With Váli, both brother and friend
Njórd, god of the sea
Skadi, giantess so free

Nanna, Baldr's own sweet lady
The just Forseti is their baby
Fulla, full of secrets of the queen
Hears things that are never seen

Eir, the best healer in the land
Strong men fall at Elli's hand
Vör, woman ever so wise
Sól and Máni rush through the skies

Hel resides down below
Völva always seems to know
Hel is the home of the dead
Where glass is sharp and feet are red

Mímir is not with Hel
Instead he is in a well
Not alive, but not quite dead
Nothing but a wise old head

Sigyn, Loki's faithful wife
Stays with him still, despite their strife
Lofn, gentle and sweet
Andhrimnír cooks the meat

Snotra is clever and keen
Kvasir's knowledge is felt and seen
Gefion built her own great farm
Hlin tries to prevent harm

Yggdrasil, a big tall tree
Home to many beasts, wild and free
Beasts that die and are reborn
Stories known by each Norn

Sjöfn stirs up matters of the heart
Sága is ever so smart
Hermódr, who always rides on
Dellingr, God of the Dawn

Fenrir, the vengeful wolf
His brother, the snake, from sea to gulf
Dwarves of east, north, south, and west
Forging great things with such zest

Dead heroes the Valkyries bring forth
Unbreakable spirits of the North
After their last earthly fall
To feast in the great old hall

Módi, Magni, and Thrúd,
Bound to Thor by his blood
Jötnar, rivals of Thor
Will aid Hel in the last great war

Thor was born of Jörd
An early giantess Nord
Heimdallr was born of nine mothers
Eight more than all his brothers

Sleipnir, the eight-legged horse
The Bífröst is his course
Narfi, Loki's son
He lost yet no one won

Dagr, God of the Day
Hœnir has not much to say
Freyja and Ódr have two daughters
But Ódr sailed away on distant waters

Hod, the one who was blind
He was tricked from behind
Aurvandill's toe is in the sky
Above where the falcons fly

So many gods to record,
Odínn, Frigg, Skadi, Njórd
Never disrespect a bard
Poetry can be quite hard

Khnum and Horus

God and god, ram and bird
Keepers of the hidden word
From Earth to Mars
Knowledge of the stars

Khnum created man from clay
So he could eat and live and play
Horus is the seeing eye
Never falls for a lie

Connected by both land and past
A ship with both sail and mast
Gods and creations forever last
Endure every worldly blast

May your heart find room
For the ancient ram Khnum
As well for falcon Horus
Who many times has come before us

Hagaar

I see, I see
The Living One has come to me
At the holy well
'Tis there, on my knees I fell

I knew then that I could rest
I knew then that I was blessed
My son and I would still live on
God can be hard to see, but He is not gone

Isis and Osiris

Isis, goddess and spring queen
Osiris, fresh again and green
Osiris killed by Seth's attack
But his wife Isis brought him back

Osiris husband and Isis wife
Endless cycle of death and life
Partners, lovers, and best friends
Their ancient story never ends

Anubis

God of the dead
With a canine's head
He is the souls' judge
From his truth he'll never budge

Like a sentry, he is loyal
Like a king, he is royal
Like a jackal, he is strong
Like the truth, he's never wrong

Tefnut and Heqet

Tefnut, mother of rain
You water the Earth and relieve its pain
Heqet, mother of land
Good things grow at your demand

Tefnut, with the head of a lioness
Your works of water do impress
Heqet, with the head of a frog
You make things grow in desert and bog

Egyptian plains
Covered in rains
Egyptian soil
Rich and royal

The mystical mystery
Egyptian history
Gods of the past
Return at full blast

Elen of the Ways

When you've been lost for days
Your pain seems to go on and on
Count on Elen of the Ways
She will guide you with her song

She will help you find your way
She and her mighty horn
She will make it all okay
She was there when you were born

She is both queen and saint
She wields a special stick
She's adorned in special paint
She comes to your rescue oh, so quick

Hair of red or hair of blonde
Grass of green and blouse of pink
Of this one I am very fond
Disappears before I blink

Wounds will heal and none shall bleed
She is there to hear your call
She'll be there in your time of need
She is with you through it all

The Eye

There I see it
The wise old eye
By lightning it's lit
Up in the sky

Angel here to dry all my tears
Eye like eternal sleep
Angel here to cleanse me of fear
When my eyes start to weep

Eye like stained glass
Thought, sight, and more
From the sky to the grass
It's clearer than before

So many eyes
Take to the skies
Take to my dreams
Comprehend beams

Open the third
See the real truth
Though it might sound absurd
It might just bear fruit

<h1 style="text-align:center">Shake</h1>

Peace of mind and the bed begins to shake
Tranquility and the bed begins to quake
Ever so lightly, gentle
Eat some acorns and a lentil

Visions

Dionysus, bald and blue
Giant dragons are there, too
Elen to guide me all the way
It seems the old ones are here to stay

A cross circled with a loving snake
All is seen for magic's sake
Deer and bats, faces swirling
Lights flash, my mind is whirling

Someone is there, I can tell
The prophecy is going quite well
Seeing things with the mind's eye
With a thankful breath I sit and sigh

The Beach

I visit the gray and cloudy beach
My blood is sucked out by a leech
My soul is sucked out by the stream
Nobody can hear me scream

Strange men sail on the water black
Could they possibly bring my soul back?
As they trudge through the murky waters
Vigorous sons and fearsome daughters

They ask me to join them on their trip
So I climb aboard their serpentine ship
Hair is washed and wood is burned
My precious soul has now returned

Oh, Ancestor

Needing much but never in need
Serpentine ship is a noble steed
Staying the same but changing course,
Oh, valiant sailor, my heart is yours

Harmless but fierce is the dragon's head
Once alive, but never dead
Large and striped is the ship's mainsail
Your voyage, our voyage, will never fail

I am the boat and you are my keel
Balance between what's fake and what's real
Through stormy seas we'll sail and we'll row
Too strong to be swept to the waters below

Ship made with skillful and tender hands
Carried across the enemy's lands
Though this story is obscure and old
It is one of the greatest ever told

Fighting for life, honor, and love
Seeking guidance from Valhalla above
Using your legs instead of your horse
Oh, berserker, my heart is yours

I truly hope for better things
My faith flies on angel's wings
I patiently wait as fate sings
I wait for the happy news she brings

Nothing bad lasts,
you know if you're clever
Now, don't be aghast,
for good is forever

My ancestors hoped for better things
No need for gold or diamond rings
The best treasures come from the heart
The heart is where we got our start

So we shall live by its rules
And one day swim in Heaven's pools

Though we have never met,
I love you just the same
Descendant of the vets
My heart is never tame

We may not dance together
Under the cold moonlight
Though we will dance forever
Through Heaven's streets of white

Some of you held an axe
Used it for attacks
To create a better life
For your children and your wife

Some of you held a hammer
To build a table strong
Though this life had no glamor
It was well and good and long

Though it is a new dawn
No matter what is said
Your memory will live on
To me you're never dead

A Great Man

He is but a peasant bard
Always turns the right card
He does not try too much
His heart is soft to the touch

He does not have cheese or lard
Doesn't have a giant feast
You might find it very hard
He does not care in the least

He does not care what you say
The good ones know that he's okay
He's careful not to walk under ladders
But he's brave when it matters

He has a friend in every town
But you're quick to put him down
Still he'd give you all he had
Because he is one great lad!

Bird Lady

Bird Lady, ancient and wild
Bird Lady, don't eat my child
Bird Lady, fly over my house
Bird Lady, don't eat that mouse

Bird Lady near my bed
Bird Lady in my head
Bird Lady waking the dead
Bird Lady, hope and dread

Bird Lady, I'll make it true
Bird Lady, I ain't scared of you
Bird Lady, let's make amends
Bird Lady, let's be friends

All was different
Yet all was the same
I know you so well
But I don't know your name

We are not like the others
We share the gift with our sisters and brothers
We can dance 'round the fire
Our spirits and voices lift higher and higher

I hope I have time to teach you these things
To help you through your pariah pains
People like us, people like you
All is special, what we feel and do

In time you will learn
As all young bairns do
You will thrive or you'll burn
But that's all up to you

Heart Beats

My heart beats, faster and faster
If I am caught, it will bring disaster
I flee from the scene
I have risked all for my queen

Oh, no! They see me!
What shall I do?
You would not want to be me
Nor would I want to be you

I trip over myself, I'm about to be caught
But my desperation sparks a thought
I keep on running
But I open my eyes
I am still cunning
But under new skies

It was all a dream
I know I am safe
I do not have to scream
I am back in my cave

My heart still pounds
And my lungs still work hard
But salvation I have found
I turned up the right card

Ode to Mom and Dad

You taught me how to be strong
What was right and what was wrong
What was wrong and what was right
You helped me gain the will to fight

You filled my eyes and heart with light
You shocked me with your royal might
You filled my ears and soul with song
I hope your lives are good and long

The woman who gave me life
Who serves me food with fork and knife
The man who puts the roof over my house
Who's never quiet as a mouse

Both guardians and friends
Your love never ends
You taught me how to be kind
Parents like you are hard to find

Ode to My Grandparents

You teach me the sacred ways
Remind me of the good old days
We revel and dance and sing
I talk your ears off till they ring

Grandma, you're the queen of cookies
Who tries to educate us rookies
Who always greets me with a smile
Who makes my life all worth while

Grandpa, you who makes me grin
When it comes to jokes, you always win
You taught me that purple is quite great
When it honors our mighty Kansas State

You've guided me for all my years
You've helped me through my hopes and fears
Your hearts and blankets so warm and wooly
It is you who have made all my holidays holy!

Wonders

Cabinet of wonders
The sound of battle thunders
Husband and wife
Trying to secure a good life

Dogs in the snow
The general orders "Go!"
Tales from another time
A grueling jungle climb

Collectors
Protectors
On the defense
It all makes sense

A teapot and a doll
Beautiful and small
A skull tattoo
That no one knew

Because of you I'm here to write
Tell of your great deeds and might
You folks fought the fight
So I could be here tonight

Poem for a Friend

Oh, my dear, dear friend
I hope I did not offend
Fate may change and time may bend
I hope our love will never end

Sometimes when I'm feeling rough,
You offer me a friendly hand
On the days when times are tough
You always seem to understand

It is you I wish to see
You know we are family
A friend like you is hard to find
So always stay cheerful, always be kind

Remember

Do you remember when we were little kids
We would sit on the couch and watch goofy vids
I wanna be like that today
I wanna laugh and joke and play

We're not growing up
We're just getting older
We're not acting up
We're just getting bolder

You're in my thoughts
You're in my dreams
You're in my loud and silent screams

Let's be friends forever more
Without you my heart would be so sore
You make me feel so complete
You're always fun and always sweet

Cater-cousins we'll forever be
When we stare out at the Twilight Tree
Blue will be red and red will be blue
I will forever more love you

For Those Gone Home

Although you are light-years away
I feel the need to say
I know you are still here
Bringing joy and banishing fear

I know you are conquering strife
Saving a life
Healing the sick
Igniting the wick

Although you are gone
Our love will go on
It always will
For love's hard to kill

You know I can see
You're watching over me
You are still giving
And you are still living

The Afterlife

I know not where we go
When this life's said and done
It's not something we can know
But I know that you're the one

It feels like such a long time
But I can stand the wait
To know I'll see your face again
At Heaven's shining gate

I do not know where I'll go
But I think I have a clue
There's one thing I do know
I'll spend my afterlife with you

Joan of Arc

All those who live must hark
The pure words of Joan of Arc
With Celtic strength and a French heart
She rode into battle to play her part

Her army was fine and strong
Her prophecies were never wrong
She helped bring forth freedom for France
In the halls of Heaven, witness her dance

One like her is hard to find
A soldier, both strong and kind
A genius with a brilliant mind
She could see while most were blind

The way she made her wise choices
Was by direction of her Voices
The archangel Michael and his ethereal host
Brought the word of the Holy Ghost

Catherine and Margaret, each a saint
Helped the holy picture paint
Though Joan was still in her youth
Her angels helped her see the truth

The Maid of Orléans, Joan of Arc
Hero of France, light in the dark
Holy one, bringer of light
Warrior, the head of the fight

❧

The one who all seek and admire
Left this world in smoke and fire
But no one can ever extinguish her flame
Jeanne d'Arc, remember that name

Saint Margaret

Saint Margaret, Queen of the Scots
Who was exiled on behalf of King Cnut's plots
Became the mother of three kings
In Paradise she now sings

Clothed in blue like Mother Mary
Inspired the towns of Queensferry
Had her own sacred cave
Her legacy is the sight of her grave

But wait, there's another story
I must tell of another's glory
Many a year before the Scottish Queen
There was another Saint Margaret to be seen

She was humble, she wasn't known for braggin'
Then she was swallowed by a dragon
She was saved by the power of her cross
Satan spited by this loss

Beheaded for her faith
"Tell my story," Margaret saith

Then there's Margaret of Castello
Sweet and kind, wise and mellow
She was put to the test
She was different than the rest

When she was born her parents lied
They told everyone that she had died
Locked her away in a hidden room
Full of loneliness and gloom

There was no doubt they were ashamed
By her their nobility had been maimed
But in truth she was Heaven sent
When she made many repent

She made a cripple learn to walk
She taught the wisdom of the Rock
Although she brought her parents strife
She lived a pious, faithful life

How many St. Margarets have there been?
It's hard to tell, but at least ten!
I guess for Margarets, that's a win
Don't even get me started on St. Catherine!

Peter the Apostle and His Host

I was trying to save a fly
I couldn't let the poor thing die
If this was right, I couldn't tell
But they let me know all was well

I was compelled to open the door
Who was it that stood before?
Peter the Apostle, in the guise of my dog
Travelling through the mist and fog

He was accompanied by elven kind
Who nowadays are hard to find
They had long hair, black shirts, and bells
I was enchanted by their spells

From Peter no speech was heard
Peter spoke not a word
Though I wished that they would stay
He and his host walked away

But although away they walked
One of the elves stayed and talked
She was sweet and kind and nice
The visit did not come at a price

That was a magical night and day
When I saw the ancient way
If you believe me, I know not
But I believe, belief I've got

Your Savior

She leads you out of the fire
Lowers you from the pyre
Banishes all your fear
The one who gifted you your spear
You are safe when she is near

You need her at all times
She gives you candies, toys, and dimes
She will heal your wounded soul
Only she can make you whole

She leads you across the perilous bridge
You will not plummet off the ridge

It was she who banished strife
It was she who saved your life!
Who is this mysterious wraith?
None other than your own faith!

Hrafna-Floki

Hrafna-Floki Vilgerdarson
Many hearts he has won
He sought neither crown nor throne
'Tis he who made Iceland a home

He was blessed with two daughters
But said goodbye to them both
One to the icy waters
One to a marriage oath

The ravens with their feathers dark
Showed him where to go, like Noah's Ark
'Twas they who gave him his name
'Twas they who gave him his fame

He arrived in Iceland with his friends and wife
There they started a new life
Springtime there was quite nice
Then came winter snow and ice

When everyone was cold and ill
He climbed up on the icy hill
He gazed upon the frozen fjord
And at the land he had explored

They say that's how Iceland got its name
The wild place is never tame
The Vikings sought to inquire
About this land of ice and fire

To get there he paid quite the price
But Floki loved his land of ice
It's true, this time, he did not stay
But he returned another day

The King

Who's that riding 'cross the field?
Who will make the Saxons yield?
Who rises up against the odds?
Who represents the Viking gods?

The heathen king, son of Ragnar
Will grow to be the North's great star!
Will slay the foe with mind and heart
Despite his dark and humble start

Travels Scandinavia and the British Isles
Charms them all with Scandinavian smiles
Who is this man? You may have guessed
None other than Ivar the Boneless!

Queen Lagertha

An ancient, wild queen
She was called obscene
By the one she loved most
Her heart was like a ghost

The Queen of wolf and bear
With long, flowing hair
Rode in to slice and slay
And then she saved the day

A Tribute to Respiratory Therapists

Do you know who's underrated?
Who's constantly degraded?
Do you know who's always forgotten?
Who stops your lungs from going rotten?

Who breathes into you a breath of life?
Who saves your parents, kids, and wife?
Just when life is at its scariest
You need a respiratory therapist

Everyone needs an RT
He'll bring you back to life with an AED
Saves a life every day
Because that's just the RT way

Cacophony

So much music to be found
Garages blare with vibrant sound
Spoons bang to keep the beat
Gongs clang out in the street

Many people wait
To end the hate
The solos are always great
Join in, don't be late!

Metal played for all to hear
Fans and friends scream and cheer
As the band breaks the barrier
The screaming folks grow even merrier

Folks blow horns and folks blow pipes
Some folks even sound like snipes
Hear the drums and hear the bass
The guitar echoes throughout the place

Join or fight, it is your choice
Many just choose to rejoice
Some say it is only noise
But it's life for girls and boys

It is a philosophy
Metal charms my heart
You call it a cacophony
But I call it art

Sandman

Hard to think clear when you're always awake
Hard to survive a massive earthquake
Hard to hope when you never dream
Hard to write a story when you have the wrong theme

Think about others before yourself
A man, a woman, a sprite or an elf
Do not listen to fibs and lies
Don't drink the poison the sick man buys

Improve your life as fast as you can
Reclaim your heritage, fight like a man
Whether you burn or whether you bleed
You will be the hero that your people need

The New Year

I'll be quiet so no one can hear
Only chaos is quite clear
They think of me as quite absurd
My thoughts are never truly heard

Ever since you left
I've been trapped in endless death
Peace is hard to find
When I'm not on your mind

I'll search for one to hold me close
A memory, a dream, a ghost
I need to banish all my fear
And patiently wait for a New Year

Yin and Yang

Sometimes I cry in the night
Life just feels like one big fight
I always must do what is right
Despite the twisted lies of spite

Things can sometimes get so scary
But I know all this is necessary
I must accept both joy and strife
To live a good and truthful life

I must keep safe those who I love
Be as wise as a snake and as sweet as a dove
Must fight off the demons at the door
I will love and fight forever more

I accept both dark and light
Both are needed for the fight
I accept both light and dark
I will become like Joan of Arc

When I feel sorrow's sharp pang
I must remember Yin and Yang
When I wonder what could have been
I must remember Yang and Yin

Wolf

I'm a wolf without a pack
A dog without a bone
A cut without some slack
A queen without a throne

I'm a lone wolf, yes
But I hate to be alone
I'm an empty chest
I'm Paul McCartney without a clone

I have the power
But I'm oh, so weak
I'm a stem without a flower
I can barely speak

I'm a deer without a fawn
They were here but now they're gone
Only you can make me whole
Only you can fill my soul

The Reason

You're the reason my heart is beating
The one who keeps my strength from fleeting
The one who's there in my times of needing
The soldier who is never retreating

Because of you my faith goes on
True love and hope are never wrong
No one is ever truly gone
You're the reason I write this song

So strong, yet easily broken
So loud, yet so soft spoken
Awake, yet not awoken
A gift, a symbol, a token

You're the frosting on the cake
Quite asleep yet quite awake
Quite awake but quite asleep
My heart is yours to forever keep

Darkness

They say dark is bad and light is good
But how can that be?
Darkness comforted me when no one else could
In the dark, I am free

Don't get me wrong, I love the light
But I love the day and the night
I love the night and the day
Duality is just my way

So when you say you're afraid of the dark
When you're wishing for a spark
Think about this cold black gift
In the cold and black, let your spirits lift

Will I Ever?

Will I ever find the one
That makes my days full of fun?
The one who'll teach me how to feel
The one who'll show me what is real?

Who will shatter my cold stone wall?
Will my heart's fortress ever fall?
Could my castle ever break?
Love is not a piece of cake

Love is such a farfetched dream
The idea of the thing makes me scream!
It seems no one can set me free
From my cold prison called apathy

I see people with their soul
They all seem to be so full
I'm sure no one can make me whole
I'm as strong and stubborn as a bull

Will Sjöfn and Lofn ever come to play?
No one will ever make me sway
Will anyone EVER change my way?
I guess I'll know it all one day

What I Think About You

You talk way too much
You do not talk enough
You're sick to the touch
Aww, you think you're so tough!

You're a coward but you act so brave
Some things you'll take right to the grave
You can't tell people how you feel
You can never be too real

You strike those you love with fear
When all you want is to spread cheer
You just need to calm a bit down
To become a person of great renown

Love and War

They say all's fair in love and war
I find nothing fair in either or
Both seem doomed from the start
Both always break my heart

But one day I will have the upper hand
Drive my enemies from my land
Have many troops at my command
Hear proud drumbeats from the band

I promise, my love,
One day we shall meet
And it, my love,
Will be so sweet

One Ancient Night

On this night
Of fear and fright
You are tasked
With wearing a mask

Beat the drum
Before they come
Chase the Beast
Into the trees

A wicker man, a ghost
Effigies to roast
Learn how it felt
To be an ancient Celt

Sprites and fairies on the scene
One ancient night, called Halloween!

Thanksgiving

The holiday we always forget
But we always still remember
The turkey in the window's lit
To brighten our home this November

Be thankful for family and friends
For food and home and God
You will hope it never ends
Eat some turkey and some cod

Remember the American brotherhood
Appreciate your brothers, too
Be thankful for all that's good
Remember, that includes you!

Eat and eat and eat some more
Watch the Thanksgiving parades
Then you can snore and snore and snore
As the family plays charades

As long as no one's sick
The whole family comes to feast
And argue about politics
Our great aunt's a beast!

But in the end, we all rejoice
Parents, cousins, and grandmothers,
Sing our thanks with heart and voice
Because we all have one another

Christmas Then and Now

Christmas comes and all is well
Angels shut the gates to Hell
Every soul is filled with joy
Because of one Baby Boy

He is the One all nations know
He was born long ago
In a land of sand, not snow
He shone with the light of Heaven's glow

Spirits dance and angels sing
With silver harps and golden wings
All the little Christmas things
Life and joy to all they bring

Everyone forgets their pain
Love and joy are the greatest gain
The best presents are still given, the wisest know how
Christmas came then, and it will come now

The Christmas Spirits

Christmas time is rolling 'round
Who comes with the jolly tide?
What wonders are to be found?
How many have *you* spied?

The special Baby in a manger
Everyone knows this one
He was born to save us all from danger
He makes the winter season fun

Reindeer, penguins, polar bears, spiders, who knew?!
Animals are part of Christmas, too
They have many special jobs to do
When Christmas time comes around, it is like a zoo!

Who protects these animals through the season's chill?
Why, the winter witch Frau Percht!
Leave her some cookies, if you will!
In the snowy fields she lurks

If you're good this Christmas, if you've been a good lad
Jolly Santa Claus will bring you gifts
But if it seems you have been bad
Krampus will give you a lift!

If you get a coat or hat
Some shiny shoes or a new dress
You will avoid the Yule Cat
He truly knows what is best

Gryla the troll has thirteen sons
They are called the Yule Lads
They're always in search of Christmas fun
Try to entertain their slothful dad

In Germany you'll likely find
An angel-girl called the Christkind
With golden wings and golden hair
You'll recognize this maiden fair

Befana or Babushka, oh, where to begin?
So many Christmas witches!
They followed the wise men
And granted children's wishes

When snow falls and blizzards blow
Welcome Jack Frost with the snow
To make sure kids are in the know
Hans Trapp appears as a scarecrow

Brownies, goblins, gnomes, and elves
Dance in your garden and sit on your shelves
Amuse them, be they good or bad
For you don't want to make them mad

Lots of snowy spirits fly
On the night of Yuletide
If you really look and spy
You'll glimpse them on their wild ride

The Snow Maiden, the Yule Goat
The Yule Log called Tió
All wear a blanket or a coat
So nobody gets frío

She may be spooky, but do not fear
When Mari Lwyd appears at the New Year
To keep the planet all in rhyme
Comes a wizard, Father Time!

Be it spirit, elf, or fairy
Joseph, sheperds, or Mother Mary
Angels sing and children play
Everyone loves Christmas Day!

Christmas Tide

Snow falls and there's an icy chill
Everyone feels an icy thrill
Remembers the great, ancient ways
Rejoices for 25 days

How the shepherds experienced a serendipity
On the holy night of the Nativity
The stars all sang with joy and might
The whole world glowed with the warmest light

How Christmas has changed over the years
With Krampus, Perchta, and other Yuletide fears
But the joy still stays the same
The wild happiness is never tame

It is better to give than to want
Spirits fly on the wild hunt
Be kind to all, be they kings, lords or peasants
And Santa might, just might, bring you presents

If you do not receive clothes,
The Yule Cat may be quite scary
As the winter blizzard blows
People listen to Mariah Carey

Christmas is a time for magic and fairies
Be careful – don't eat the holly berries!
It's a time to celebrate
To let in love and banish hate

As long as you believe
You'll have a merry Christmas Eve
Every child and every sprite
Will rejoice on Christmas night

The Wild Hunt

See the haunts on the wild ride!
Wise old Odin and his cunning bride
The lady known as Frigg
Followed by sprites both small and big

Giant goats and sleek black horses
Fairies in coats and otherworldly forces
Every ghost and every goblin
Is on the hunt, floatin' and wobblin'

Frau Perchta is shaking her sheets
The one who demands treats
From all those she meets
Cookies, candy, and beets

Thor rides by, bringing thunder
Specters of all kinds join in on the plunder
Gwyddion, Baldr, and Herne the Hunter
All who see them are in wonder

Who is all involved in this wild chase?
Who knows? Perhaps, Elen of the Ways!
Queen Medb, searching for a cow
I can almost hear them now

On cold winter nights when you hear a loud howl
Don't blame it on wind or a friendly old owl
Blame it on spirits on the hunt
If they knock at your door, give them what they want!

What do you want? What do you need?
Does your mind succumb to greed?
On Christmas, what do you ask for?
Gold and silver, more and more?

Ask for sunshine, ask for snow
Pray for those that dwell below
There are things that money can't buy
A beauty that you can't deny

On your birthday when you wake up
Do you want ice cream and a cake cup?
Or do you want each heart to find true love?
The moon and stars to shine above?

Do you wish for peace, wish for grace,
Wish for a smile on each face?
Or do you need a fancy dress?
Do anything just to impress?

I know what I wish for
Love and joy, from sky to floor
The world can be so much more
Better than it was before

We can be so much more
If we ask for less
We are not poor
We are already blessed

Change

Purity is hard to find
Psychologists don't help your mind
How did we all become so blind?
Why can't we all be true and kind?

Change your ways, turn to light
Lengthen your days, exile spite
Change your life, embrace the dark
Feel the night, set off a spark

It all depends on you
How you act and what you do
Don't always follow what you're told
Save the lives, both young and old

Don't get me wrong, listen to others
Consider our wise sisters and brothers
But you must realize the whole truth
To unite the lands like old Bluetooth

You never know what really goes on
When you are not there
Your opinions could be wrong
Seek the truth, if you dare

Beauty or the Beast?

Do you ever try to change the world?
Do you even dream?
You make my eyelashes want to curl
You make my mouth want to scream

Who is the bad guy,
Hades, or Zeus?
If you listen to the lie
You might get confused

Hephaestus is a beauty
Aphrodite is a beast
A large ham is a poverty
A small crumb is a feast

Did Arke deserve to lose her wings?
Do you hear the words the angel sings?
Wonder why villains do what they do?
Perhaps the answer has always been you!

Why is the monster under your bed?
Why is the demon on your chest?
Why can't the walking corpse stay dead?
Maybe it is for the best

Always do the right thing
I am tired of your behavior
Let bells of compassion ring
Be kind to your neighbor

Know every little creature
Knows how to love and feel
Know magic is life's teacher
And it is very, very real

Message to Tyrants

You stole, you stole, you stole our land
And now, tyrant, you shall fall at our hand
You took all that's ours and made it your own
Worked us to the very bone

We will drive you far away
The time has come, it is today
We shall be free as in times of old
The story of rebellion shall be told

We will do what is necessary
When we are mad we can be quite scary
The battle has come, the battle is nigh
The wings of the valkyries help us to fly

Our people will be safe, our people will be free
It is up to us, it is up to me
No tyrant shall walk where the rebels stand
No tyrant can drag us from our land

We Will Not Comply

All the land is up in fire
We will not be this satire
Make me look like a liar
But we are something to admire

Make us look like a joke
See our dreams go up in smoke
Make me feel like I could choke
Strangled by this lying cloak

We will not comply
We are still alive
We will never die
You know we'll survive

You can't stop us now
And you never could
We will never bow
We'll fight for all that's good

You think we'll believe this
What a silly thought
Ignorance is bliss
But sometimes it is not

You've got war hawks like peace doves
We've got faith, hope, and love
You've got smoke to blind and smother
We're better off, for we have each other

We will never let you stop us
We're not cowards, we're not weak
If we fight, we know we must
It is freedom that we seek

The Poem

Lord of All
Father of the large and small
He is the First, He is the Last
He is the Future, Present, and Past

Hair like snow
Eyes like fire
Made the rivers flow
He is for all to admire

The Father, Son, and the Holy Ghost
He is Lord of the Holy Host
He is Father of the Sky
He assures we shall not die

It is He who shall save the day
All you have to do is pray